ideals CHRISTMAS

Vol. 46, No. 8

Publisher, Patricia A. Pingry
Executive Editor, Cynthia Wyatt
Art Director, Patrick McRae
Production Manager, Jeff Wyatt
Editorial Assistant, Kathleen Gilbert
Copy Editors, Marian Hollyday
　　　　　　　 Rhonda Colburn

ISBN 0-8249-1078-8

IDEALS—Vol. 46, No. 8 December 1989 IDEALS (ISSN 0019-137X) is published eight times a year: February, March, May, June, August, September, November, December by IDEALS PUBLISHING CORPORATION, Nelson Place at Elm Hill Pike, Nashville, Tenn. 37214. Second class postage paid at Nashville, Tennessee, and additional mailing offices. Copyright © 1989 by IDEALS PUBLISHING CORPORATION. POSTMASTER: Send address changes to Ideals, Post Office Box 148000, Nashville, Tenn. 37214-8000. All rights reserved. Title IDEALS registered U.S. Patent Office.

SINGLE ISSUE—$4.95
ONE-YEAR SUBSCRIPTION—eight consecutive issues as published—$17.95
TWO-YEAR SUBSCRIPTION—sixteen consecutive issues as published—$31.95
Outside U.S.A., add $6.00 per subscription year for postage and handling.

ACKNOWLEDGMENTS

CHRISTMAS IS A STATE OF MIND by Mary Ellen Chase. Courtesy *Vogue.* Copyright © 1938 by The Conde Nast Publications, Inc.; THE INNKEEPER'S LAMENT and LET US KEEP CHRISTMAS from *THE ETERNAL THINGS* by Grace Noll Crowell. Copyright 1942 by Harper & Row, Publishers, Inc. Renewed 1970 by Reid Crowell. Reprinted by permission of Harper & Row, Publishers, Inc.; YOUR CHRISTMAS GUEST by James Dillet Freeman from *BEST LOVED UNITY POEMS,* 1956. Used by permission of the Unity School of Christianity, Missouri; ON GOING HOME FOR CHRISTMAS from *EDGAR A. GUEST BROADCASTING.* Copyright 1935, The Reilly & Lee Co. Used by permission; THE MAN WHO GAVE US CHRISTMAS, Copyright © December 1939, Winifred Kirkland, as first published in *The Atlantic Monthly.* Reprinted by permission; OUR HOUSE, SO FULL OF CHRISTMAS from *EARTHBOUND NO LONGER.* Copyright 1961 by Caroline Eyring Miner. Used by permission; THE WISER WISE MAN from *CHRISTMAS COULD-BE TALES (And Other Verses)* by Margaret C. Rorke. Copyright 1984 by Northwood Institute Press, Midland, MI. Used by permission of the author; MORNING SURPRISE from *SOMETHING BEAUTIFUL,* Copyright 1966 and TILL CHRISTMAS COMES AGAIN and THE GIFTS WE GIVE by Garnett Ann Schultz. Used by permission. Our sincere thanks to the following whose addresses we were unable to locate: Virginia Covey Boswell for DECEMBER SONG; Angela E. Hunt for CHRISTMAS IN AMERICA; Bernadette Kernen for SANTA'S LAP; Nancy Nowiszewski for CHRISTMAS DREAMS; Mary Reas for IT'S COMING CHRISTMASTIME; Thelma I. Stegeman for CHRISTMAS.

The paper used in this publication meets the minimum requirements of American National Standard for Information Sciences—Permanence of Paper for Printed Library Materials, ANSI 9.48-1984

Typesetting by The Font Shop, Nashville, Tennessee

Color Separation by Rayson Films, Inc., Waukesha, Wisconsin

Printing by W.A. Krueger Company, Brookfield, Wisconsin

Front and back covers　　Photo Opposite
　　Dick Dietrich　　　　SANTA'S WORK

WINTER BLESSING

Evelynn Merilatt Boal

I looked out on a wonderland this morning:
Each branch and twig precisely etched with frost.
White filigree adorned the lamps and railings;
The windowpanes with new lace were embossed.

And as the sun peeped warmly from its covers,
Then rose to touch each icy scene it found,
Bright jewels sparkled everywhere it ventured—
On frozen bush and spilled on snowy ground.

Each season offers some unique enjoyment.
The Spring brings green, and Summer has its glow;
While Autumn covers woods and walks with colors.
But Winter gives us diamonds in the snow.

Morning Surprise

Garnett Ann Schultz

I found the world this morning
Neath a blanket pure and white;
The snow so soft and gentle
Had fallen through the night.
No footprints marred its loveliness,
No earthly thing was there;
And only wintertime supreme
Had made the whole world fair.

I found the trees this morning,
Each one dressed in splendor true
With every branch all covered
By the nighttime snow so new.

How lovely was the hilltop
In the early morning dawn,
Just before the world awakened
As the nighttime fast was gone.

I found the world this morning
And I thought it quite a thrill,
As the precious little snowflakes
Brought a charm to yonder hill.
It was pleasant at the dawning,
And my heart was filled with charms
When I found the world this morning
Snug and safe in Winter's arms.

Photo This Page
SUMAC IN THE SNOW
CHEATHAM COUNTY, TENNESSEE
Mack & Betty Kelley

Seamstress

Loretta Bauer Buckley

Dame Nature stitched
With immaculate thread
A coverlet
For every bed;
She tucked the rose
Soft and deep,
Whispering gently,
"Sleep now, sleep."
O'er grass she wove
With fingers white

A cover of down—
Velvety, light.
Embroidering each tree
With ermine strand,
She stitched and stitched
With tireless hand.
Each withered stalk
Of flower became
A silver taper
With a silver flame.

DECEMBER SONG

Virginia Covey Boswell

December wind has flung its gathered chills
Beyond the swooping sleds on winter hills
And sent the red scarves whipping frosty air
Around the throats of laughter sounding there.
Now twilight tastes of snow that's coming soon,
And chimney smoke curls toward a coin of moon;
Inside, the gift of warmth, hot chocolate calls,
With plates of homemade cookies shared by all.
Candles at the windows welcome friends
Who stop to chat before the season ends;
The mailbox fills as Christmas Day appears,
With messages that bridge the miles and years;
And wonder lights the stars throughout the skies
For children holding Christmas in their eyes.
It's to December memories belong—
Whose windy music writes a timeless song.

8

Photo Opposite
A LIGHT IN THE WINDOW
Dick Dietrich

It's Coming Christmastime

Mary Reas

When you feel that bit of friendliness
Where before it wasn't found,
When you see a warmth within a smile
Where once there was a frown,
You know at once it's almost here,
It reflects in song and rhyme,
And love is felt throughout the world:
It's coming Christmastime.

When you're shoved and jostled in a crowd
And your patience grows quite thin,
Someone might whisper, ''Pardon me,''
And you'll feel that glow again.
There's something magic happening,
No mistaking in the sign;
When folks begin to love again,
It's coming Christmastime.

You'd love to give to everyone
No matter what the cost.
You think of all the friends you've made
And regret the ones you've lost.
The wind is cold against your skin
Yet all is warm inside,
Because the world's in love again:
It's coming Christmastime.

Photo Opposite
THE GRAND AVENUE MALL
Rouse-Milwaukee, Inc.
MILWAUKEE, WISCONSIN
Henry J. Hupp/Laatsch-Hupp Photo

LET US KEEP CHRISTMAS

Grace Noll Crowell

Whatever else be lost among the years,
Let us keep Christmas still a shining thing;
Whatever doubts assail us or what fears,
Let us hold close one day, remembering
Its poignant meaning for the hearts of men;
Let us get back our childlike faith again.

Wealth may have taken wings, yet still there are
Clear windowpanes to glow with candlelight;
There are boughs for garlands and a tinsel star
To tip some little fir tree's lifted height.
There is no heart too heavy or too sad
But some small gift of love can make it glad.

And there are home-sweet rooms where laughter rings;
And we can sing the carols as of old.
Above the eastern hills a white star swings;
There is an ancient story to be told;
There are kind words and cheering words to say.
Let us be happy this glad Christ Child's day.

Photo Opposite
CHRISTMAS LIGHTS ON CARSON MANSION AT DUSK
HUMBOLDT COUNTY, CALIFORNIA
Jeff Gnass Photography

Our House So Full of Christmas

Caroline Eyring Miner

Our house, so full of Christmas, is bursting at the seams,
For every little corner is full of Christmas dreams.
The dresser drawers are bulging; they scarcely can be shut.
The fruitcakes, fully ripened, are begging to be cut.

The basement now resembles a special kind of zoo,
For rugs conceal strange bundles that almost frighten you.
Our house is wrapped in Christmas—the tinsel fairly gleams
Along the roof's low edges where icicles catch the beams
From candles burning brightly upon the mantel shelf,
That spit and sputter merrily, each like a Christmas elf.

And if I were blindfolded and couldn't see a thing,
My nose would tell me ''Christmas'' and make me want to sing.
And if I only heard the sounds that come from everywhere,
I'd know that it was Christmas that filled the very air!

The candy mixture bubbling, the popcorn's steady beat
Against the lid, the crackle of pine logs throwing heat
To every nook and cranny where someone has a hoard
Of neatly wrapped surprises that he could ill afford;
And mother singing softly, and father chuckling low,

The children's shy swift glances a-counting so and so.
There's not a tiny corner that isn't brightened up.
Our house is running over with Christmas like a cup.
I'm glad our house is big enough and small enough in one
To keep this Merry Christmas until the year is done.

Photo Opposite
THE MAGIC OF CHRISTMAS
Larry Lefever/Grant Heilman

Christmas Feasting

Cornish Game Hens with Wild Rice

Makes 4 servings

½ cup butter *or* margarine
½ pound fresh mushrooms
1 medium-size onion, diced
1 large clove garlic, crushed
½ cup walnut halves
4 Cornish game hens (1 to 1¼ pounds each)
¾ cup wild rice
4 chicken bouillon cubes
2 cups water
Salt and pepper to taste

Clean mushrooms; remove stems and slice. In a large skillet melt 2 tablespoons butter *or* margarine. Add mushrooms, onion, garlic, and walnuts and sauté lightly. Remove from skillet and set aside. Clean hens inside and out; pat dry. Truss legs to body of each hen. Add remaining butter *or* margarine to skillet; brown hens on all sides over medium heat. Wash rice; in medium-size bowl combine rice, bouillon cubes, and water. Reduce heat under skillet and add rice mixture. Spread evenly under and around hens. Cover and cook at a slow simmer for 45 minutes or until hens are tender. Remove hens from skillet. Crisp hens breast-side up 4 to 5 inches from broiler, if desired. Add mushroom mixture to rice; salt and pepper to taste.

Herbed Vegetables

Makes 6 to 8 servings

6 cups assorted vegetables
¼ cup chicken stock
⅛ teaspoon salt
1 tablespoon dried basil
½ cup finely chopped fresh parsley
½ cup finely chopped scallions *or* green onions

Steam vegetables until tender-crisp. Heat chicken stock in large skillet. Add salt, basil, parsley, and scallions; mix. Stir in steamed vegetables. Heat to serving temperature and serve immediately.
Note: Suggested vegetables are carrots, yellow squash, peas, red peppers, broccoli, and cauliflower. Cut into bite-size pieces.

Florentine Scalloped Potatoes

Makes 6 servings

1 10¾-ounce can condensed Cheddar cheese soup
1 16-ounce can tomatoes, drained and chopped
1 10-ounce package frozen chopped spinach, thawed
½ cup sliced onion
1 tablespoon chopped fresh parsley
½ teaspoon lemon juice
½ teaspoon marjoram
1 clove garlic, minced
Dash pepper
2 cups shredded Swiss cheese, divided
4 cups thinly sliced potatoes

Preheat oven to 375°. Butter a 2-quart casserole. In a mixing bowl, stir together all ingredients except ½ cup cheese and the sliced potatoes. In the prepared casserole, layer sauce alternately with potatoes, beginning and ending with sauce. Cover; bake 1 hour and 10 minutes. Uncover; sprinkle with reserved cheese. Bake an additional 15 minutes.

Mincemeat Pie

Makes 6 servings

Pastry for a 2-crust pie
2 cups mincemeat
½ cup orange marmalade
2 tablespoons flour
1 tablespoon lemon juice
¼ teaspoon nutmeg
1 tablespoon butter *or* margarine
Milk
Sugar

Roll out half of the pastry on a floured surface to a circle 1 inch larger than an inverted 9-inch pie pan. Fit into pan; set aside remaining dough. In a mixing bowl, combine mincemeat, marmalade, flour, lemon juice, and nutmeg. Stir to blend. Turn into pie shell. Dot with butter; set aside. Preheat oven to 425°. Roll out remaining dough; cut into lattice strips. Weave strips over top of pie; trim strips and press firmly to edge of bottom crust. Brush lattice with milk; sprinkle with sugar. Bake for 35 minutes or until crust is golden brown.

Christmas Is a State of Mind

Mary Ellen Chase

During those confusing days before Christmas, while I wrap gifts for sisters and brothers, nephews and nieces, aunts and friends, I remember my grandmother who, in the twenty years I knew her, wrapped Christmas gifts for no one at all. She viewed with fine scorn all the Christmas frenzy of gift buying and gift giving. "Christmas, children," my grandmother would say, "is not a date. It is a state of mind."

To be sure, she spent most of her waking hours making things for others—yards upon yards of tat-ting, hundreds of tea-cosies, table mats, hemstitched handkerchiefs, knitted stockings, mittens, and shawls. They were all gifts, yet they were never given at Christmas. Instead, they were presented at odd moments to all sorts of persons—to the gardener, the minister's wife, a surprised boy coasting down the hill, the stage driver, a chance peddler, the fishman.

My grandmother's nature was essentially dramatic. She loved blizzards, northern lights, falling stars; she loved all sudden, unexpected things. But she loved them only if either she or God instigated them. She was distinctly irritated if anyone took her unawares either by a sudden gift or by an unexpected piece of news. She was so filled with life herself that she forever wanted to dispense rather than to receive. Since she liked to engender excited surprise in those about her, her big objection to Christmas lay in the fact that it was a day of expectation when no one could possibly be taken by surprise.

Unlike most women, she scorned possessions; and she saw to it that she suffered them briefly. We knew from the beginning the fate of the gifts we annually bestowed upon her. Yet, following the admonition of our parents, from our scanty Christmas allowance we set aside a portion for Grandmother's gift. She received our offerings without evident annoyance, knowing that what she must endure for a brief season she could triumph over in days to come.

My grandmother waited for a fortnight or longer after Christmas before she proffered her gifts to family, neighbors, and friends. By early January, she concluded, expectation would have vanished and the rapture of sudden surprise might again be abroad in the world. Around three o'clock on some dreary afternoon, she would set forth. Over her coat she tied a stout black sateen apron, and in its capacious lap she cast all the gifts that had come to her unwanted—odd bits of silver and jewelry, gloves, handkerchiefs, books, perfumes, knickknacks of every sort. She would return at suppertime, empty-handed and radiant.

As we grew older and were allowed to select our gifts free from parental supervision, we began to face the situation. Instead of black silk gloves for Grandmother, we chose for her our own favorite perfumery; we substituted white handkerchiefs for the black-edged ones which she normally carried; a box of chocolates took the place of peppermints; a book called *Daily Thoughts for Daily Needs* was discarded in favor of a novel.

Grandmother has long since gone where possessions are of no account, but I still receive from time to time the actual return of her Christmas gifts so curiously dispensed. Only last Christmas a package from a friend revealed a silver pie knife marked with Grandmother's initials and presented to her, I remembered with a start, through the combined sacrificial resources of our entire family fully thirty years before. An accompanying note bore these words: "Your grandmother brought this knife to my mother twenty-eight years ago as a Christmas gift. I remember how she came one rainy afternoon in January with the present in her apron. I found it recently among my mother's things, and, knowing your grandmother's strange ways as to Christmas gifts, I am returning it to you."

Tied to the pie knife by a bit of aged red ribbon was a card inscribed on one side: *To Grandmother with Christmas love from her children and grandchildren,* and on the other: *To my dear friend, Lizzie Osgood, with daily love from Eliza Ann Chase.* ✳

Mary Ellen Chase was professor of English at Smith College at Northhampton, Massachusetts, for twenty-nine years and was the recipient of numerous awards and honorary degrees. She wrote children's books, essay collections, novels, textbooks, and contributed stories and reviews to newspapers and periodicals. She was often praised for the warm humanity of her characters.

Christmas Dreams

Little one, my little one,
With big blue eyes so bright,
What wondrous dreams will fill your mind
On this glorious Christmas night?

Will you be seeing dolls and games,
Or a rocking horse so real
That you'll ride it to the hilltops
Where fairies dance at will?

And should you stop to join them
In their merriment so true,
I have but one small favor
That I must ask of you:

You may ride your horse to hilltops,
You may dance with fairies too,
But please return to Mother,
Whose own dreams live in you.

Nancy Nowiszewski
Des Moines, Iowa

What Is Christmas?

Twinkling tree lights and mantelpiece stockings,
Wreaths with red berries and visitors knocking,
Ornaments sparkling like stars in the skies;
Christmas is laughter and cheer and surprise.

Mistletoe kisses and bright fires glowing,
Carolers singing and goodies o'erflowing,
Packages wrapped up and placed round the tree;
Christmas is friendship and music and glee.

Letters to Santa and warm, hearty greetings,
Jingling sleigh bells and families meeting,
The joy of the season is ours to give.
Christmas is LOVE; in your heart may it live!

Mary Agnes Seabrook
Mt. Pleasant, South Carolina

Reflections

Perfection

I love a good snowstorm, my dreams to inspire,
A nice wintry day to sit by the fire
And visit my book friends whom so long I've neglected
Or write that letter someone has expected.

It's a fine day to embroider, to mend, or to sew
And watch Mother Nature knit a blanket of snow.
Each flake is a stitch very dainty and light,
Transforming the earth with a blanket of white.

I don't know how many she knits or purls;
Sometimes the flakes come down in great swirls,
Covering the branches of each lovely tree,
Knitting a cover of lace filigree.

Each tiny flake of glistening white
Dances and sways like an elfin sprite.
A spectacle of beauty is each fencerow and ditch,
The blanket is perfect, though she dropped every stitch.

Gladys Manes Kidwell
Knoxville, Tennessee

Editor's Note: Readers are invited to submit
unpublished, original poetry, short anecdotes,
and humorous reflections on life for possible
publication in future *Ideals* issues. Please send
copies only; manuscripts will not be returned.
Writers receive $10 for each published submission.
Send material to "Readers' Reflections," Ideals
Publishing Corporation, P.O. Box 140300,
Nashville, Tennessee 37214-0300.

The Point

"Tis the season to be jolly!"
So the story goes.
Why is it, then, that everybody
Seems to have the woes?

Could it be their hearts and minds
Just cannot seem to find
The time to stop and focus
On the Savior of mankind?

For that's what Christmas is, you know.
The blessed, holy birth
Of God, the Father's only Son,
Who came to save the earth

From all this worry, rush, and hassle
That we seem to think a must.
When all our loved ones really want
Is our friendship, love, and trust.

So share the greatest gift of all,
Wrapped as a baby boy
Who will never need replacing
Like a sweater, tie, or toy.

"Tis the season to be jolly!?"
Well, yes! But better, still,
Is the joy unspeakable in our hearts
That only Christ can fill!

Alice Allen
Dayton, Ohio

MCRAE.

CHRISTMAS IN AMERICA

Angela E. Hunt

Ah, Christmas. This festive season of merriment and gratitude has been celebrated throughout the world for nearly 2,000 years. In the past 300 years, a distinctly American Christmas has taken shape: a melding of the traditions which the early settlers brought with them when they settled in the New World. Christmas as we know it today is a crystallization of miracles and gifts, reindeer and camels, solemn masses and feasting.

Most of our customs came with the early English colonists in New England and Jamestown. The Jamestown settlers wrote of their first Christmas in the New World in 1607: "The extreme winds, rayne, frost and snow caused us to keep Christmas among the savages, where were never more merry, nor fed on more plenty of good Oysters, Fish, Flesh, Wild Fowl and good bread, nor never had better fires in England." If there has ever been any question as to the role of women in the celebration of Christmas, let these early days stand for the record: this was a strictly male feast with none of the decorations or trimmings, because there were no women in the colony initially. The first truly festive Christmas was held in Jamestown in 1619, when ninety women arrived at the settlement.

As Jamestown prospered, the English settlers became known for their hospitality and Christmas merriment. The pleasure-loving English people brought such customs as the ringing of bells, burning of a Yule log, playing of games, and singing of carols. Evergreens decorated their homes and churches, and candles in abundance shone through the night.

Unlike the all-male Jamestown settlers, the families among the 102 settlers who founded the Plymouth Colony anticipated the spirit of Christmas and brought barrels full of ivy, holly, and laurel with

The Bettman Archive

them on the Mayflower. The decade which the Pilgrims had passed in Holland to escape religious persecution in England had taught them Dutch traditions, and they decorated tables, mantels, and doors with chains and wreaths made from fir branches. Dutch traditions also included the exchange of gifts and feasts of turkey, pudding, and pie.

The later Puritan settlers frowned on the celebration of what they considered to be a pagan festival, the tide of Yule, an ancient pre-Christian observance which included stage shows, caroling, gaming, and other merry-making, elements deeply entrenched in English Christmas customs. When the Puritans realized that the celebrations of Christ and Yule were inseparably intertwined, they cast out the entire holiday. To show their disdain, they planned hard work for December 25 and a law was passed forbidding the celebration of Christmas. By 1659 the General Court of Massachusetts felt it necessary to enact a law establishing a fine of five shillings on those who observed Christmas Day. This law was repealed in 1681, but it was not until December 9, 1686, that a Christmas service was conducted in Boston under legal sanction. No New England college had a Christmas holiday until as late as 1847, and Christmas remained a workday until 1856. The atmosphere in New England changed gradually, but not until 1856 was the day made a legal holiday in Massachusetts. As late as 1870, schools held classes on December 25. It is ironic that one thinks of a "New England Christmas" as the most time-honored and traditional, when in fact it was the southern colonies that kept Christmas without interruption from those early beginnings in the New World.

A distinct input in American Christmas celebrations comes from Germany through the Moravians, whose households in Pennsylvania and North Carolina prepared the traditional Kuemmelbroad, sugar cake, mince pies, and Christmas cookies. On Christmas Eve families attended the "love feast" at church, where a good-sized bun and large cup of coffee were served to all as a token of fellowship. Before the end of the church service, a lighted wax candle was passed to each person and the house lights darkened to remind him of the coming of the One who is the light of the world. This visually moving tradition is celebrated in various churches in America to this day.

In the early days of Christianity, the birthday of Jesus was celebrated as a feast day as were the birthdays of Christian saints. The European Christmas calendar gradually spread from December 25, the agreed-upon date of the birth of Jesus, to a twelve-day period which concluded on January 6, observed as both the day of Jesus' circumcision as an infant, the visit of the Wise Men to Bethlehem, the miracle of Cana, and Jesus' baptism at the age of thirty. (It is also the date of St. Nicholas' death in A.D. 342.) This twelve-day holiday period carried over to America and was a special time for the signing of treaties and for weddings. In our young nation's history, George Washington married the widow Martha Curtis on Twelfth Day, January 6. Thomas Jefferson married Martha Skelton on New Year's Day in 1772. Although our modern world is too busy for twelve days of holiday, Christmas is still considered a very special time for weddings.

Christmas trees are relative newcomers to the American Christmas, but the Christmas tree tradition is an ancient one stretching back to ancient Teutonic cultures where the enduring vitality of the winter evergreen was emblematic of the immortality of the soul. Christmas trees in America were first found in the Moravian church's communal settlement at Bethlehem, Pennsylvania, in 1747. These were not real evergreen trees but the European style of wooden pyramids covered with evergreen boughs and flowers. The trees were decorated with popcorn chains, gilded nuts, frosted cookies, paper dolls, ribbons, berries, and fruits. Small candles in gilded egg cups shone from every limb. When Queen Victoria married Prince Albert almost a hundred years later in 1840, he brought the Christmas tree to England, where its popularity quickly spread.

Not everyone in America was thrilled with the Christmas tree's popularity, however. In 1883 a *New York Times* editor criticized the tree, calling it "a rootless and lifeless corpse—never worthy of the day." He predicted that the Christmas tree would fade in popularity while the more traditional Christmas stocking would endure.

Ironically, central heating and automatic clothes dryers have made obsolete the common practice of hanging one's damp socks to dry overnight at the hearth where one morning a year they might be found stuffed with treasures; but the hearty symbol of hope blooming eternal in the midst of winter, the Christmas tree, may well be the most indispensable ingredient to the modern family Christmas in America.

A very merry American Christmas to you all!

———————————— ✳ ————————————

Angela E. Hunt, a native Floridian, is a youth pastor's wife with two children. She has published several children's books and also writes for teenagers and about parenting and child-rearing. She enjoys quilt making.

Christmas Remembered

Janice E. Hinkle

Smelling Christmas cookies baking,
Licking spoons from candy making,
Helping tie a package bow
With finger placed upon it so,
Greeting friends at wreath-trimmed door,
These and many, many more
Are things that we remember.

Shining eyes and candlelight,
Big new bikes with paint that's bright,
Stifling a sleepy yawn,
When tykes awake at crack of dawn,

Wrappings strewn across the floor,
These and many, many more
Are things that we remember.

Shining star that led the way
To Jesus sleeping in the hay,
Reborn hope of Jesus' birth
Bringing peace and joy on Earth,
Golden angels' wings that soar,
These and many, many more
Are things we should remember.

The Man Who Gave Us Christmas

This inspiring story about the apostle Luke was published in the Atlantic Monthly *fifty years ago in December 1939. Its timeless message is still of value to all who celebrate Christmas.*

Winifred Kirkland

An eminent doctor, Luke also excelled in painting and sculpture. This painting, attributed to Raphael, shows the evangelist painting a portrait of Mary and the infant Jesus.

How many of us in the hurry and hubbub of the holiday season steal a few silent moments to consider where our Christmas comes from? Stories as beautiful as that of Christmas do not just happen; they have a source, they come from somewhere, they come from someone. When we stop to think and search for a sure but distant origin, we shall find, contrary to the evidence of this mass-mad decade, that over and over again some far-off individual, man or woman, is responsible for giving the whole world some undying dream, a dream that can always be seen to have been long and courageously preserved within the dreamer's own undaunted soul. Yet this far-off bravery too often fails to stir us, because we seldom pause to look back and remember.

From year to year we join in the singing of the old familiar carols, forgetting who recorded the very first Christmas hymns that have set the fashion for all that have followed. From year to year we listen while some voice reads, My soul doth magnify the Lord, without remembering how high and holy and humble some far-off man must have kept his spirit before he could have perceived the ineffable loveliness of the Annunciation and shared a young mother's glory in a child-to-be. Every year we gather together, young and old, to construct the Christmas crèche. We arrange the sheep, we place the kneeling shepherds, we crown with a halo the baby's head lying on the straw, but we forget the man who so revered the sacredness of commonplace things that he dared to describe a God laid in a cattle trough for a cradle. We forget the man who gave us Christmas.

We do not know Luke well enough to say thank you to him across the centuries. But we might know him better, and Christmas might mean more to us, if we tried to discover what it must first have meant to the man who gave it to us, gave it in all its perennial freshness and beauty to a world racked with war in his day and still racked with war in our day, in spite of the soaring, singing message of the two thousand Christmases that have come between. While in no sense did Luke invent the Christmas narrative, one can with truth say that it was he who gave us Christmas, for it was Luke, and Luke only, who searched out and found and preserved a birth story too humble for prouder historians to touch. It is said of Jesus, the wayside preacher, that the common people heard him gladly. It may be said of Luke, the wayside doctor, that he heard the common people gladly. Was it these same common

26

people who brought to Luke's knowledge the story of the first Christmas, revealing to him perhaps the existence of some close-kept Aramaic document, or simply transmitting to him by word of mouth sacred and secret memories? The narrative of Jesus' birth seems to have been unknown to the earliest Christian Church, concentrated as that church was on its Founder's death and Resurrection. Who else but humble people, still open to wonder and awe, could have told those old tales of miracles and angel voices? Who else but Luke would have listened? Who else in that day and hour reverenced humanity enough to accept the story of a God born in a stable and to give that story to the world?

Let us read once again the first two chapters of Luke's Gospel. Then let us pause to consider where our Christmas comes from, picture by picture, chant by chant. The most beautiful book in the world, so Renan has described the Gospel of Luke. And in that book, for sheer unearthly loveliness, the opening chapters are the most beautiful of all. Only a painter could have conceived the strange stark beauty of the scene in which the tall angel delivers his message to a wondering awestruck girl. In fact, some early statues of Luke represent him as an actual artist, carrying palette and brushes. Only a dramatist could have seen and made us see that doorway meeting of two rapt women, one young, one old, each bearing beneath her heart a little child. Only a man attuned to music like a harp could have given us those immortal chants uttered by Zechariah and Mary and Simeon. . . .

. . . We possess little enough information about Luke, but it seems to be generally accepted that he was a young doctor of Antioch and a member of the Christian community there before he met Paul and joined that intrepid leader on his second missionary journey as his personal physician. . . . Paul's description of his friend has become part of the world's vocabulary: "Luke, the beloved physician."

. . . It was the "beloved physician" who could describe motherhood in all the holiness of our Christmas narratives. It was one who had given all his being to the service of others, and who was never to hold a child of his own in his arms, who could set down the raptured words: "My soul doth magnify the Lord." It was one whose life was consecrated to the relief of suffering who could describe with such exaltation Jesus' miracles of healing. Long before he had ever heard of the mysterious man executed in a distant city, Luke, a joyous-hearted young Greek, must have chosen a career of kindliness. He had himself gone about doing good before he was equipped to write of all the wealth of kindly deeds and sympathetic words that he records in his life of Jesus. Of all four Evangelists, it is Luke who best reveals Jesus the man, friend always of the poor and the downtrodden, comforting even the despairing thief crucified beside him, as Luke alone tells us. It is a joyous human Jesus that Luke presents, probably because he himself had learned high joy in his close contact with an unseen Master. In spite of all its tragedy, Luke's Gospel gives the reader a sense of unconquerable gladness, gladness like that of the two disciples on the walk to Emmaus when their Master returned to share a meal with them, an incident that Luke alone has saved from oblivion. Truly Luke was mysteriously fitted to transmit to us forever the joyousness of Christmas.

. . . Thus there came into existence a book which to this day presents the supreme appeal of Christianity to all paganism past or present. The universality of the Christian faith is revealed by the fact that Luke's book was written by a Greek to a Roman about a Jew.

. . . But what had these sacred stories of a holy little child meant to Luke himself in his darkening old age, in his darkening world? Persecution was rife. For all we know, Luke may have written in the very shadow of his own martyrdom; some ancient authorities say that he was martyred. From end to end of Palestine the armies of Rome had gone raging and avenging. No one could count the fallen dead that Luke's pen might have recorded but did not. Instead, Luke, an old unbroken man, sent forth from the stricken world of his day to our stricken world of today the deathless hope of an angel hymn, and the deathless promise of a newborn child.

Christmas Contentment

Dan A. Hoover

Come join us this year at the fireside
And warm to its crackling glow,
While winds of midwinter moan under
   the eaves
And pile up the new-fallen snow.
Sister will fix us some popcorn
With butter like warm, melted gold;
And Brother will go to the cellar
For apples, red, striped, and cold.
Grandma will rock at her knitting;
How swiftly her worn fingers go!
While Mother ties bows on last-minute gifts
And adds to the tree's treasure-trove.
Grandpa is napping, his hands in his lap,
Seed catalogs spilled on the floor.
He sees the long rows of green, growing
   things
When summer comes gently once more.
Dad's reading the paper but now and then
   smiles,
As love binds us closely and fills
Our hearts and our home with the spirit
   of Christ
As His star shines down on the hills.

29

Photo Opposite
THE CHRISTMAS HEARTH
S. Barth/H. Armstrong Roberts

A Slice of Life

Edgar A. Guest

On Going Home for Christmas

He little knew the sorrow that was in his vacant
chair;
He never guessed they'd miss him, or he'd
surely have been there;
He couldn't see his mother or the lump that
filled her throat
Or the tears that started falling as she read his
hasty note;
And he couldn't see his father, sitting sorrowful
and dumb,
Or he never would have written that he thought
he couldn't come.
He little knew the gladness that his presence
would have made
And the joy it would have given, or he never
would have stayed.
He didn't know how hungry had the little
mother grown
Once again to see her baby and to claim him for
her own.
He didn't guess the meaning of his visit
Christmas Day,
Or he never would have written that he couldn't
get away.

He couldn't see the fading of the cheeks that
once were pink
And the silver in the tresses, and he didn't stop
to think
How the years are passing swiftly, and next
Christmas it might be
There would be no home to visit and no mother
dear to see.
He didn't think about it—I'll not say he
didn't care.
He was heedless and forgetful, or he'd surely
have been there.
Are you going home for Christmas? Have you
written you'll be there?
Going home to kiss the mother and to show her
that you care?
Going home to greet the father in a way to
make him glad?
If you're not I hope there'll never come a time
you'll wish you had.
Just sit down and write a letter—it will make
their heartstrings hum
With a tune of perfect gladness—if you'll tell
them that you'll come.

*Edgar A. Guest began his illustrious career in 1895 at
the age of fourteen when his work appeared in the Detroit
Free Press. His column was syndicated in over 300
newspapers, and he became known as "The Poet of the
People." Mr. Guest captured the hearts of vast radio
audiences with his weekly program, "It Can Be Done,"
and, until his death in 1959, published many treasured
volumes of poetry.*

Christmas As It Used To Be

E'lane Carlisle Murray

Across the shadowed room, still bright
Against the dark enclosing night,
Is a merry fire and curling smoke,
Crackling with mesquite and oak.

In a corner, cool and dim,
Its branches bright with tinsel trim,

Standing straight for all to see
Is the cedar Christmas tree.

Above each door, with ribbons red,
Sprigs of mistletoe are spread.
Soft green leaves and berries white
Reflect the candles' golden light.

Long brown stockings in a row,
Dark against the golden glow,
Hang near the soft and gray ash bed
Warmed by embers burning red.

Children dream while in each toe
A golden orange is sure to go!
And crammed with wonders to the top,
Their ribbed expanse will all but pop.

A top that spins and sweetly sings,
A harp to blow, a bell that rings,

A jackknife, or a baby doll,
A red and bouncy rubber ball.

Between these treasures, here and there,
Pecans and walnuts everywhere,
And brightly striped in red and white,
Sweet sticks of peppermint to bite.

The years may pass and yet they'll stay
And never wholly go away.
I can close my eyes and see
Christmas as it used to be.

A Stable Boy's Christmas

Little Joshua awoke with a start as the broom came down upon his thin back. "Come on! Up with you or I'll have the caravan cart you off to market!" The innkeeper's wife scolded the lad until he was standing. "Now here's your breakfast and don't dawdle about eating it. There's lots to do and the day is flying!" The heavily built woman handed Joshua a hunk of cold lamb roast and a slab of coarse bread, then hurried back to her busy kitchen.

Joshua wolfed down the food, wiped his greasy fingers on his homespun tunic and set about his morning chores. He was an orphan, but one of the lucky ones, for he had a place to sleep at night and a source of food and companionship. Bethlehem was not kind to her street children and Joshua was grateful to the innkeeper and his wife for taking

him on as a stable boy. He didn't mind their harsh ways; life was hard and he accepted that. Besides, he loved the kindly animals he tended. He talked with them as he brushed and fed them, embraced their warm and obedient necks, and he was comforted by their soft breathing as he fell asleep each night.

The recent days had been hectic as the census had increased the town's population several-fold. The innkeeper was delighted with the influx of patrons, but his wife was almost driven to distraction by the additional meals and cleaning, and Joshua was kept running from dawn 'til dark, tending the camels, donkeys, and horses left in his keeping by the many guests. As long as he kept busy, did his job, and remained out of sight, his life was uncomplicated, if lonely. But he had learned not to expect much from life, and so was not easily discouraged. It was true, however, that he longed, from time to time, for a family; for a mother's soft caress, a father's proud embrace. But those thoughts brought pain so, for the most part, he drove them from his mind with busyness.

It was late in the afternoon and he had just finished clearing the stable floor of the animal droppings and stale straw and was busy scattering fresh hay on the stone floor when sounds of an argument drew Joshua's attention. In the entryway of the inn, a man and a woman, dusty and weary looking, were talking with the innkeeper.

"But I tell you I have no room. There is nothing. Go on now." Joshua recognized the deep voice of his employer rising in intensity.

"But you must take them, Simon," his wife countered. "Look, the poor woman is pregnant. You can't cast her out in the streets! The sun is about to set."

The object of the discussion drooped in the afternoon heat. She looked as if she might fall off of her poor, exhausted donkey at any moment. Something about her attracted the stable boy's attention and, quite unconsciously, he slowly walked to the entryway.

What happened next was quite unexpected and Joshua never knew what possessed him to do it, but, in a rush of compassion, he reached for the donkey's lead and, taking it in his hand, said, "I'll find them a place. The stable is clean and dry and it will at least be quiet and off the street."

The innkeeper and his wife stared at Joshua with astonishment and for a moment he thought he would be struck for his brashness. But then the innkeeper shrugged his shoulder and motioned his wife to go inside. "If that suits you, go with the lad," he offered brusquely, dismissing them with a wave of his hand.

Joshua led the couple and the little donkey back to the freshly cleaned stable, piled a deep mound of straw in the corner, and helped the grateful woman spread her cloak upon it. Then he left them alone and took the dusty beast outside, watered and fed him, and brushed his matted coat. Sometime before midnight the weary stable boy fell into a deep sleep, lulled by the night breezes and the warm familiar scents of the contented animals.

It was still dark when Joshua awoke and he lay still, disoriented by the suddenness of his awakening. There was an unusual sensation about the night—it was as if the air had a different texture, the night sounds a different tone. Silently, he crept toward the place where he had left the two strangers the night before and, peeking over the edge of a wooden corral, he saw them sitting together in a pool of light. Through an opening in the stable's roof, the light of a single brilliant star flooded into the dark chamber. In its light, Joshua saw a tiny hand move. The woman was holding a newborn baby, cradling him in her arms. She was humming softly and the father of the child looked on quietly.

It was a scene from one of Joshua's daydreams—a loving mother, proud father, adored child. The beauty of it pierced the lonely child's heart and a sob escaped. Hearing the sound, the young mother looked up and caught sight of the little spy.

"Come," she whispered. Her look of tenderness and love drew Joshua from his hiding place. He came and knelt beside her, peering at the little infant in her arms. "What is your name, child?"

"Joshua," the stable boy replied.

"Well, Joshua, this is Jesus. Do you know that is the Greek form of your name? It means 'God is my salvation.'"

Joshua just shook his head. He hadn't known his name meant anything. He hadn't known that *he* meant anything.

"Would you like to hold him?" the mother offered.

Speechless, Joshua held out his grubby arms and gently took the child. He cradled the infant near his heart and watched the tiny lips smile in sleep. He felt his own heart beating loudly in his ears and heard the woman's words echo in his mind: "God is my salvation."

It was as if the star's clear light had shone into his soul and illuminated it with hope. He touched the baby's flawless cheek with a tender gesture and knew in a knowledge born of faith that although he was alone, he would never be lonely again. Here in the dark and silent stable, among the homely animals and sweet straw, Love had sought out a little orphan boy. ✳

Pamela Kennedy is a freelance writer of short stories, articles, essays, and children's books. Married to a naval officer and mother of three children, she has made her home on both U.S. coasts and currently resides in Hawaii. She draws her material from her own experiences and memories, adding bits of imagination to create a story or mood.

The Annunciation

And in the sixth month the angel Gabriel was sent from God unto a city of Galilee, named Nazareth, to a virgin espoused to a man whose name was Joseph, of the house of David; and the virgin's name was Mary.

And the angel came in unto her, and said, Hail, thou that art highly favoured, the Lord is with thee: blessed art thou among women. And when she saw him, she was troubled at his saying, and cast in her mind what manner of salutation this should be.

And the angel said unto her, Fear not, Mary: for thou hast found favour with God. And, behold, thou shalt conceive in thy womb, and bring forth a son, and shalt call his name JESUS. He shall be great, and shall be called the Son of the Highest: and the Lord God shall give unto him the throne of his father David: and he shall reign over the house of Jacob for ever; and of his kingdom there shall be no end.

Then said Mary unto the angel, How shall this be, seeing I know not a man?

And the angel answered and said unto her, The Holy Ghost shall come upon thee, and the power of the Highest shall overshadow thee: therefore also that holy thing which shall be born of thee shall be called the Son of God. . . .

And Mary said, Behold the handmaid of the Lord; be it unto me according to thy word. And the angel departed from her.

And Mary arose in those days, and went into the hill country with haste, into a city of Juda; and entered into the house of Zacharias, and saluted Elisabeth. And it came to pass, that, when Elisabeth heard the salutation of Mary, the babe leaped in her womb; and Elisabeth was filled with the Holy Ghost; and she spake out with a loud voice, and said, Blessed art thou among women, and blessed is the fruit of thy womb. And whence is this to me, that the mother of my Lord should come to me? For, lo, as soon as the voice of thy salutation sounded in mine ears, the babe leaped in my womb for joy. . . .

And Mary said, My soul doth magnify the Lord, and my spirit hath rejoiced in God my Saviour.

Luke 1:26-47

FERRY DE CLUGNY ANNUNCIATION
Van Der Weyden (1400-1464)
Metropolitan Museum of Art

The Wiser Wise Man

Margaret Rorke

They call me "Casper," one of three
Who rode on camel back
Across the desert's sandy sea
To bring a treasure pack
Of frankincense and myrrh and gold
To place before a king,
The kind of gifts in days of old
A worshipper would bring.

We found the King, an infant child,
Not in a palace bed,
But with His Mother, meek and mild,
Within a lowly shed.

We knelt and gave Him what we'd brought,
Expecting no return,
Yet from His countenance we caught
What wise men have to learn:

Though man may give symbolic gifts,
They never can compare
With what God gives and how it lifts
The hopes and fears all share.
We saw His Son—a baby boy,
And, as we took our leave,
He gave His Gift—the gift of joy
All mankind may receive.

The Innkeeper's Lament

Grace Noll Crowell

They told me afterward there was a light
That shone night long above my khan's
    low roof,
Centering above the stable, radiant, white;
They tell me now it was a heavenly proof
That the Christ whom we had waited for
    so long
Was there . . . that I had turned Him from
    my door.
They say above the fields there was
    a song
Such as mankind had never heard before.

How could I know—how could I hear or see
Other than the clamor of the crowd,
The bleating sheep, the bartering cries, the queer
And sharp demands upon me that were loud?
If they had only told me! If they had,
I would have turned the other guests away.
I believe that everyone would have been glad
For the stable's shelter and a bed of hay
To give the Christ Child room . . . Oh, surely I
Shall not be known forever as the one
Who shut his ears to a woman's needy cry,
Who closed his door upon God's holy Son.

The Babe in the Manger

And it came to pass in those days, that there went out a decree from Caesar Augustus, that all the world should be taxed. (And this taxing was first made when Cyrenius was governor of Syria.) And all went to be taxed, every one into his own city. And Joseph also went up from Galilee, out of the city of Nazareth, into Judaea, unto the city of David, which is called Bethlehem: (because he was of the house and lineage of David:) To be taxed with Mary his espoused wife, being great with child.

And so it was, that, while they were there, the days were accomplished that she should be delivered. And she brought forth her firstborn son, and wrapped him in swaddling clothes, and laid him in a manger; because there was no room for them in the inn.

And there were in the same country shepherds abiding in the field, keeping watch over their flock by night. And, lo, the angel of the Lord

NATIVITY
Paolo Schiavo (1397-1478)
John G. Johnson Collection
Philadelphia Museum of Art

40

came upon them, and the glory of the Lord shone round about them: and they were sore afraid. And the angel said unto them, Fear not: for, behold, I bring you good tidings of great joy, which shall be to all people.

For unto you is born this day in the city of David a Saviour, which is Christ the Lord.

And this shall be a sign unto you: Ye shall find the babe wrapped in swaddling clothes, lying in a manger. And suddenly there was with the angel a multitude of the heavenly host praising God, and saying, Glory to God in the highest, and on earth peace, good will toward men.

And it came to pass, as the angels were gone away from them into heaven, the shepherds said one to another, Let us now go even unto Bethlehem, and see this thing which is come to pass, which the Lord hath made known unto us. And they came with haste, and found Mary, and Joseph, and the babe lying in a manger. And when they had seen it, they made known abroad the saying which was told them concerning this child. And all they that heard it wondered at those things which were told them by the shepherds.

But Mary kept all those things, and pondered them in her heart.

Luke 2:1-19

ADORATION
Attributed to Paolo Schiavo (1397-1478)
John G. Johnson Collection
Philadelphia Museum of Art

The Golden Carol

Old English Carol

Of Melchior, Balthazar, and Gaspar, the
Three Kings of Cologne.

We saw the light shine out afar
On Christmas in the morning,
And straight we knew Christ's Star it was,
Bright beaming in the morning.

Then did we fall on bended knee
On Christmas in the morning,
And prais'd the Lord, who'd let us see
His glory at its dawning.

Oh! ever thought be of His Name,
On Christmas in the morning,
Who bore for us both grief and shame,
Affection's sharpest scorning.

And may we die (when death shall come),
On Christmas in the morning,
And see in heav'n, our glorious home,
The Star of Christmas morning.

The Christmas Gifts

Anna D. Lutz

Sweet Mary leaned against the hay
Beside His manger bed;
Strong Joseph kept his silent watch
And praying, bent his head;
The night wind ceased its sighing,
But softly whispering, said,

Peace!

The light burst forth from heaven
And swept away the night;
The startled shepherds knelt
And saw the vision burning bright,
Heard the message of salvation,
Knew the meaning of the light:

Hope!

The angels o'er Judeah's plains
Set all the earth to singing;
The weary world rejoiced to rise
And set the bells to ringing;
Responding to the gift of Life,
The Christ to us came bringing:

Joy!

These gifts from God we pray for all
As Jesus's birth draws near,
May you receive His Peace, His Hope,
The message of good cheer
From heaven itself, the gift sublime
That sweetly crowns the year:

Christmas!

Madelyn Stanchfield Trobilcock

Photo Overleaf
MARBLE FORK
SEQUOIA NATIONAL PARK
CALIFORNIA
Ed Cooper Photo

CHRONICLE
— Lansing Christman —

December is my natal month, and this year I join the ranks of the octogenarians. Having been accorded this span of eighty years, I have a lot of Christmastimes to remember. I do not know, of course, how old or how young I was at the first Christmas celebration I am able to recall, but Christmas has always been special in our house. There is much to remember, to cherish and enjoy, and I still remember when there was a jolly old Santa Claus in my life.

There were no lavish gifts in our childhood. We did not expect them. Our Christmases on the stony hill farm where our family lived were frugal ones, but they were filled with joy. A visit from Santa Claus rewarded our hope and expectancy with a book, a brightly colored top that would spin and hum, an orange, a candy cane, and clothing. The happiness of those many Christmas days still shines in my recollections.

We never failed to bring in a tree from the woods

and decorate it with ornaments that gleamed in the lamplight's glow. We made pinwheels, using paper, straight pins, and clothespins.

One of the most treasured of my early memories is an old railroad swamp my mother called the "Christmas marsh" because it was lush with black alder bushes. Glistening in the sun or shining and sparkling in their silvered coats after a freezing rain or draped in winter's pristine snow, they garbed the drab marsh in a festive display of emerald leaves and ruby-red berries. As a boy, I went with her to gather sprigs of those bright berries to use as decoration for our farmhouse. The beauty of the season, then and now, is full of miracles such as this, the discovery of life and loveliness in the midst of a wintry sleep.

Despite the great number of Christmastimes I have known, I find that the spiritual meaning of the holiday has grown richer with each December. With greater wisdom, we envision the Wise Men following the star in the east to the manger in Bethlehem where Christ was born. We sense more deeply the essence of this holy day as we sing our praises to God for his gift of everlasting life, a gift that will in time swing open the gates of the heavens for our entrance into the dawn of a new and glorious day.

The author of two published books, Lansing Christman has been contributing to Ideals *for almost twenty years. Mr. Christman has also been published in several American, foreign, and braille anthologies. He and his wife, Lucile, live in rural South Carolina where they enjoy the pleasures of the land around them.*

THE TWO TREES

Beulah Sutton Waite

We have two Christmas trees this year.
One stands shining and tall
In the living room for all to see.
The other is down the hall
In a room where the children like to play;
And this one they claimed as their own.
Just what trimmings this tree should wear
Was for them to decide, alone.

Small willing hands worked long and hard
To string ropes of popcorn just right,
With, here and there, some cranberries red
Mixed in with the snowy white.
Little red stockings for Santa to fill
Were placed on some branches, low.
Peppermint canes by their handles were hung,
And nuts wrapped in bright foil aglow.

Cutouts from colored paper too,
Some old but well-loved toys;
Yes, odd decorations but close to the hearts
Of these dear little girls and boys.
Our big tree is trimmed with myriad lights
And a glistening star high above;
But the children's tree is prettier far,
For they trimmed it with special love.

Photo Opposite
BRINGING HOME THE TREE
R.C. Paulson/H. Armstrong Roberts

BITS &

Christmas Trivia

Why are the three magi who visited the infant Jesus sometimes called the three kings of Cologne?

Helena, mother of Constantine the Great, the Christian Emperor who ruled the Roman world three hundred years after the death of Christ, preserved the remains of the three magi in Constantinople. At the time of the Crusades, the remains were transferred to Cologne Cathedral by the Emperor Barbarossa, and the Archbishop of Cologne adorned the relics with jewels. Henceforth the magi were referred to as the three kings of Cologne.

What is the origin of our custom of erecting nativity scenes, or crèches, at Christmastime?

The first crèche is attributed to Saint Francis of Assisi, who assembled a facsimile manger scene complete with livestock, believing it would help his congregation to find inspiration in the story of the birth of Jesus. The fodder from his re-created mangers was thought to have medicinal charms and was preserved for use throughout the year.

The New Year

'Twas a package left from Christmas—
    Left beneath the tree a week—
One we couldn't shake or open,
    Couldn't even take a peek.
Now that we've removed the wrapping,
    We are still in some dismay
'Cause we can't be sure what's in it
    'Til we've used up every day.

Margaret Rorke

PIECES

For us, however, in these northern climes, and with our traditions and associations, Christmas could not well be better placed than where it is. Nature is in slumber, as if in death—fit picture of the sleep of man till roused to righteousness by the voice of the newborn Babe of Bethlehem. Life is at its lowest, and death reigns, or seems to reign, everywhere. Saving the thick-berried holly, the mistletoe, dear to Druid priests, the laurel, and the yew, the trees are bared, and the warblers of the sky avoid their desolate branches. We are driven inward. The fireside is the centre of a thousand charms. Home is clothed in its most beautiful garments. We are forced to the conclusion that we need other help than Mother Earth can give us. Our hearts open instinctively to heaven and its message, and with willing feet we haste to do the will of Him "Who, though He was rich, yet for our sakes became poor."

David Gregg, D.D.

It is good to be children sometimes, and never better than at Christmas when its mighty Founder was a child Himself.

Charles Dickens

Rise, happy morn; rise, holy morn;
Draw forth the cheerful day from night:
O Father, touch the east and light
The light that shone when Hope was born.

Alfred, Lord Tennyson

A good conscience is a continual Christmas.

Benjamin Franklin

Some say that ever 'gainst that season comes,
Wherein our Saviour's birth is celebrated,
The bird of dawning singeth all night long;
And then, they say, no spirit dares stir abroad;
The nights are wholesome; then no planets strike,
No fairy takes, nor witch hath power to charm,
So hallowed and so gracious is the time.

William Shakespeare

Rightly has Christmas been made the children's festival. Every child is a saviour, who is come to save us from degrading ambitions, and to take us by the hand and to lead us to pleasanter fields and sweeter pastures than those which we, by our cunning and craft, have made for ourselves. They know better than we what is good for the soul; they are nearer than we are to the life of things.

Temple Scott

Illustration by Frances Hook

Santa's Lap

Bernadette Kernen

I like to visit Santa Claus
When Christmastime is near.
It's fun to climb up on his lap
And whisper in his ear.

He says, "My dear, have you been good?
Have you done what Mother said you should?
Do you brush your teeth and hair each day?
Are you kind to others when you play?"

I listen to each question
And answer every one.
Although I am ashamed to say
I must say no to some.

But Santa never scares me;
He doesn't even scold.
He just says, "Try again, my dear,
You're a fine lad, I am told."

Gee, I like to visit Santa Claus
When Christmastime is near.
It's fun to climb up on his lap
And whisper in his ear.

FROM MY
G·A·R·D·E·N
JOURNAL

Deana Deck

Happy Holly Days

One of my favorite sights in the winter landscape is that of a snow-covered holly laden with berries, playing host to an assortment of chickadees, tufted titmice, and elegant cardinals.

Certain plants are irrevocably associated with holidays, and the holly is certainly a traditional component of the Christmas celebration. Its glossy green leaves and bright red berries are a popular motif in wrapping paper and greeting cards and lend a touch of seasonal color to arrangements for decorating mantelpieces and dining tables. It's also frequently pressed into service as personal decor: a sprig tucked into a buttonhole or pinned to a collar brightens up anyone's holiday attire.

Holly, of the species *Ilex*, is found throughout the world and, in addition to its use at Christmas, has played a part in medicine, magic, science, and legend in cultures as diverse as those of ancient Egypt and Syria, China and South America.

Although long symbolic of Christmas revelry, the holly's history as a holiday decoration reaches back into the pale mists of antiquity and predates the Christian celebration by hundreds and perhaps even thousands of years. Many contemporary customs concerning holly date from the early Druid superstitions and beliefs.

Because of holly's propensity for retaining its leaves and rich color for weeks, even months, after being cut, the Druids believed that it was inhabited by woodland spirits who continued to live in its branches. The kindly Druids cut holly branches so that these spirits could pass the winter indoors.

The Romans also incorporated holly into their high winter celebrations. Many customs of Saturnalia, the ribald year-end festival honoring Saturn, god of Seedtime and Harvest, were eventually absorbed into early Roman Christian observances of Christ's birth, even though the use of pagan ritual decorations was originally forbidden.

When the Romans invaded the British Isles in 55 B.C., their holiday use of holly coincided nicely with the prevailing Druid customs, and when Christianity became established, holly continued to be the sentimental favorite for decorating dwellings and churches.

In this country, European explorers as early as A.D. 1536 recorded accounts of Indians brewing tea from the leaves of the yaupon holly for medicinal purposes. The plant's high caffeine content makes it an effective emetic, as its botanical name, *I. vomitoria*, implies.

Hollies are easily grown, acid-loving plants requiring an environment much like the azalea, although they prefer full sun. They should be grown in rich, high-humus soil which drains well; and they should be planted rather shallowly, so that the top of the root ball is higher than the surrounding soil. In areas with heavy clay soils, it is best to plant the holly above ground in a mound of more porous soil.

Holly is popular in the landscape for use in hedges, barriers, screens, as specimen and accent plants, as well as for ground cover, foundation and background plantings, and shade and boulevard trees. Hollies vary in size from the tiny dwarf varieties that only grow to one or two feet to the majestic tree-sized American holly which reaches forty to sixty feet in height. A major shortcoming is that most species are only hardy to Zone 6, which includes both coasts and continues in a general line across the country taking in the southern halves of Pennsylvania, Ohio, Indiana, Missouri, Oklahoma and most of Arizona and New Mexico. One very attractive and popular variety is the Chinese holly, which is hardy to Zone 7.

There are both spiny- and smooth-leaved varieties available with red, black, or orange berries. The majority of holly varieties have both male and female plants and require the presence of both sexes to produce berries. It is best to buy a named female cultivar, which is the sex that bears berries. Many hollies that fail to bloom simply need a mate.

Hollies are extremely popular with birds for both food and shelter and are often planted to attract songbirds and other wildlife. While not often considered as a shade tree, the larger varieties are useful for shading a hot window or porch. In hot weather, Gypsy, my elderly golden retriever, frequently seeks cool shelter under the dense branches of our large American holly.

The best time to prune a holly is anytime after the new growth of spring has hardened off. I only prune mine in winter. Timing this chore to coincide with the beginnings of the Christmas holiday season will give you masses of rich, dark green foliage laden with berries for making wreaths and arrangements —if you get there before the birds do!

Deana Deck's garden column is a regular feature in the Sunday *Tennessean.* Ms. Deck is a frequent contributor to Nashville *magazine and grows her Christmas hollies in Nashville, Tennessee.*

The Many Faces of Santa Claus

*T*he collector of Santa Claus images will find a fascinating history behind the various apparitions which the bearded old gentleman for whom children wait with such anticipation has taken over the years. The history and development of the distinctly American Santa can be traced with the help of paper collectibles: the many nineteenth-century illustrations for "A Visit from St. Nicholas" (or *The Night Before Christmas* as it is also known), postcards which were a popular way of sending Christmas greetings as late as 1926, and advertising. All of these show the path which has led to our present-day Santa Claus.

Santa Claus, one of the most universal figures of our time, was like many other famous persons born in obscurity. Like many other distinctly American traditions, he has roots in other countries, other times.

Our modern-day Santa had his beginning in real life as St. Nicholas, born in Patara, Lycia (today part of modern Turkey), around A.D. 270. Nicholas began his acts of charity and kindness as a child; his parents were wealthy and he distributed this wealth to the poor and needy secretly, usually at night.

Legend says that he supplied the dowry for three sisters by throwing a bag of gold through their open window. The gold landed in a stocking hung up to dry, and the tradition of leaving gifts in stockings was born.

Nicholas was ordained bishop, performed many miracles in his lifetime, and became the patron saint of and bearer of gifts to children in Holland, Germany, France, and Austria. He was described as having a white beard, wearing the red robes of a bishop and the traditional bishop's hat, and carrying a shepherd's crook. In Holland and Germany he was portrayed traveling on a white horse, while in other areas on foot or by goat or on a donkey.

In these early days of Christianity, the birthdays of saints were celebrated as feast days. St. Nicholas Eve, December 5, became a traditional time for the distribution of gifts in honor of his December 6 birthday.

After the Protestant Reformation in Northern Germany, St. Nicholas was replaced by the *Krist Kindl*, the Christ Child, represented as a young girl dressed in white and wearing a crown of candles. By this time, gifts were exchanged on Christmas Day and St. Nicholas had become a servant to the *Krist Kindl*. He wore simple fur robes and cap and acquired the name of *Pelz Nichol*, Nicholas in Furs. Eventually, *Krist Kindl* was to be Americanized as Kriss Kringle, which remains an alternative name for the red-clad elf with the white beard.

When they landed at New Amsterdam, the Dutch brought with them their beloved St. Nicholas. The Dutch called St. Nicholas *Sinterklass*, *Sancte Claus* and *San Nicolass*. He rode above the rooftops in a wagon drawn by a white horse, dropping gifts down the chimneys of good girls and boys.

In 1644 New Amsterdam fell to the British and became New York. *Sancte Claus* was Anglicized to Sante Claus and later Americanized to Santa Claus. By the time Clement Clarke Moore wrote "A Visit from St. Nicholas," in 1822, Santa Claus was a familiar figure. In Moore's poem, which is a true American classic, St. Nick changed from a dour, benevolent saint to a jolly old elf. "A Visit from St. Nicholas" is considered one of the greatest pieces of word painting in the English language. Never before did St. Nicholas ride in a sleigh drawn by eight tiny reindeer, each with a name; reindeer which carried him over the rooftops of the world on Christmas Eve. Never before did he get into the homes of good little boys and girls by going down chimneys. He had become an American original, Santa Claus.

Thomas Nast, a German immigrant and artist, laid the visual foundation for our modern-day Santa in a series of Christmas drawings for *Harpers' Weekly* from 1863 to 1866. Nast drew Santa as both a gnome-like figure and also as a man of normal height. He was the first to portray Santa as the "jolly, round-bellied, white-bearded, fur-clad embodiment of good cheer" as described in "A Visit from St. Nicholas."

He was also the first to put Santa in a red, skin-tight, fur-trimmed suit, drawing on his boyhood memories of *Pelz Nichol*. This illustrated *Santa and His Works* appeared about 1867. The Santa we know today, with his more loosely fitting red suit with white fur trim evolved from Nast's version of Santa.

In 1931, Haddon Sundbloom painted a life-size Santa which the Coca-Cola Company used in their advertising. He combined the characteristics given to Santa by Moore and Nast. Although he was no longer "a jolly old elf," he was "chubby, plump, and had twinkling eyes."

Sundbloom's Santa became a model for other artists. Today when we hear the words "a jolly old elf," Kriss Kringle, or St. Nick, we picture, knowingly or not, Sundbloom's Santa Claus, the real Santa for millions of children around the world. It is his Santa who is eagerly anticipated, who comes down the chimney to fill the stockings. It is Sundbloom's Santa who, each year, renews in us the spirit and hope of Christmas.

Eugene Fazekas

Eugene Fazekas is a professional photographer whose interest in Santa Claus images has resulted in an extensive collection of cards, books, and even music boxes. He and his wife reside in northern Pennsylvania.

The Gifts We Give

Garnett Ann Schultz

The gifts we give at Christmas
Can be wrapped in papers bright
With a big red bow that sparkles
In the still of Christmas night;
The many toys and playthings
That the little ones adore,
The fun and games we cherish
With the children, on the floor.

The gifts we give our children
Can be presents much more grand
If we'd give them more in patience
Or with loving, helping hands;
Time for books and time for dreaming,
Friendly moments after school,
To listen to their questions,
Let them help to make each rule.

Life can hold a special blessing
If we'll lend a patient ear,
Teach them loving and believing,
Sometimes dry a bitter tear,
Ever doing things together,
Sharing moments rich we live.
The things that money cannot buy
Are the nicest gifts we give.

CRAFTWORKS

Something Special for the Christmas Tree

These charming tree ornaments are easy to make, will make wonderful presents, and will be very welcome at tree-trimming time.

Rocking Horse Ornament

Materials Needed:

2 packages of ⅛- to ¼-inch gold trimming braids in two different styles for saddle trim and harness

Colored felt—choose three contrasting colors for body, rocker, and upper saddle

Crewel yarn for mane and tail in color of your choice

2 x 1½-inch muslin strip

2 x 1-inch muslin strip

Craft glue

Polyester fiberfill

Black sequins for nostrils

Star sequins and tiny black beads for eyes

Constructing Mane and Tail:

Step 1: For the horse's mane, fold the one- by one-half-inch muslin strip in half lengthwise and iron lightly for a sharp fold line. Thread a crewel needle with crewel yarn, pull to double strands and stitch loops closely together along the fold line. Loops should be one inch long. Reinforce the fringe at the base with a running stitch in matching thread and cut the loops open at the top. Trim fringe so that it is even and roughly three-quarters of an inch long.

Step 2. Use same procedure to produce the half-inch wide, one-inch long tail.

Constructing Horse:

Step 1: Pin pattern to felt and cut out. Position the two horse pieces with wrong sides together and position the mane between the two dots shown on pattern so that muslin does not show, observing the stitching line at base of ears. Note: Ears will be free-standing with fringe between them anchored at stitching line. Running-stitch in place. Anchor the tail in place using the same method. With a blanket stitch in matching thread, stitch horse together, leaving an opening where the saddle goes; stuff with fiberfill; and sew to close.

Step 2: Apply glue to the tabs of Saddle A, and glue onto horse. Glue the smaller Saddle B onto the larger saddle, and glue gold trim onto Saddle B.

Step 3: Apply gold trim with glue for harness, using photograph as a guide.

Stitching Rocker and Finishing:

Step 1: Stitch sides and bottom of rocker. Stuff *lightly* with fiberfill.

Step 2: Sew the horse's legs into the rocker and finish blanket-stitching to close.

Step 3: Glue on two star sequins for eyes and small black sequins for nostrils. To finish, glue tiny black bead in center of each star sequin.

60

Photo Opposite
Gerald Koser

CRAFTWORKS

Angel Ornament

Materials Needed:

Colored felt in two contrasting colors plus white
  felt for face
Craft glue
Polyester fiberfill
One package gold edging trim
Three gold sequins for buttons
One red sequin for mouth
Black and red embroidery thread

Instructions:

Step 1: Pin pattern to felt and cut out. Blanket-stitch the head together, leaving one-third-inch opening at the bottom of the head.

Step 2: Blanket-stitch the wings together and glue on gold edging trim. Fasten wings to the inside of the back of the body so that wings begin at the neckline.

Step 3: Blanket-stitch back and front of body together at the sides, leaving both the top peak and bottom open.

Step 4: Insert the top peak of the body into the opening at the base of the head. Stitch the head to the body, using a small running stitch.

Stuffing and Finishing:

Step 1: Stuff head and body with fiberfill and blanket-stitch the bottom of the body until closed.

Step 2: Sew angel's face on the head with a running stitch. Glue gold braid around head to make the halo. Embroider the eyes with one strand of black embroidery thread using a small backstitch. For the nose, embroider two French knots with one strand of red embroidery thread. For the angel's mouth, glue half of a red sequin in place. Sew gold sequins down front of angel for buttons.

Note: Use heavy-weight gold thread to make loops for hanging the ornaments on the tree.

Clara Zuspann

Mrs. Clara Zuspann has been creating Christmas tree ornaments as gifts for her family for years. She makes her angels and rocking horses in Evansville, Indiana.

Want to share your crafts?
Readers are invited to submit original craft ideas for possible development and publication in future Ideals *issues. Please send query letters (with photographs, if possible) to Editorial Features Department, Ideals Publishing Corporation, P.O. Box 140300, Nashville, Tennessee 37214-0300. Please do not send craft samples; they cannot be returned.*

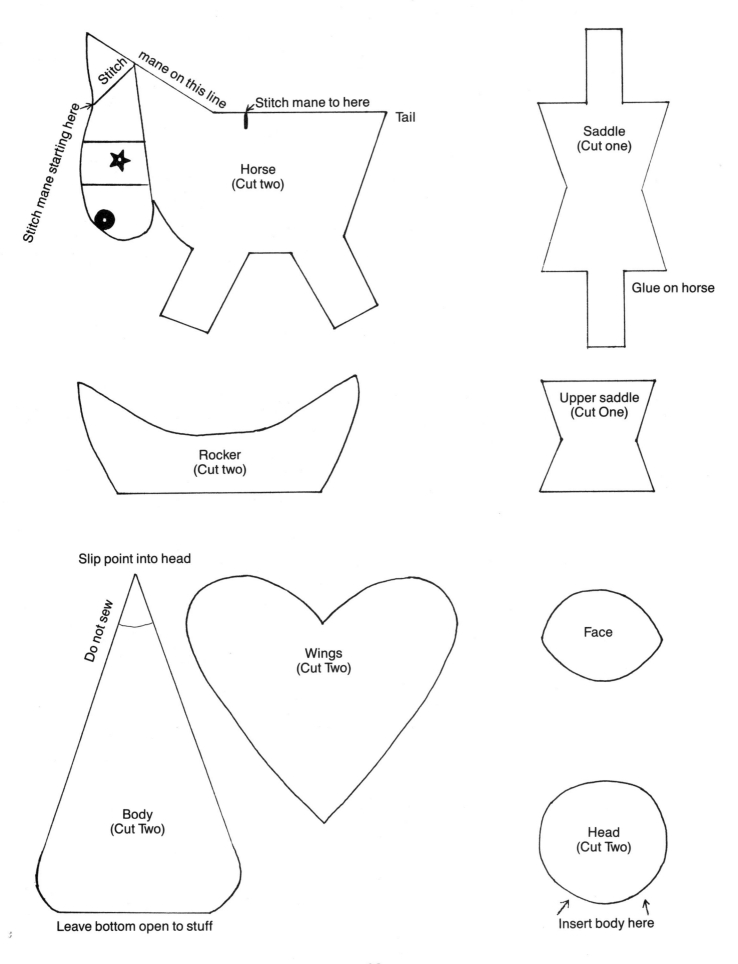

Stitch mane starting here

Stitch mane on this line

Stitch mane to here

Tail

Horse
(Cut two)

Saddle
(Cut one)

Glue on horse

Rocker
(Cut two)

Upper saddle
(Cut One)

Slip point into head

Do not sew

Body
(Cut Two)

Wings
(Cut Two)

Face

Head
(Cut Two)

Leave bottom open to stuff

Insert body here

Christmas

Thelma I. Stegeman

We used to go to Grandma's house
When it was Christmastime,
Partway by train and part by sleigh—
The sleigh was most sublime.
Uncle, clad in fur, would drive
His horses in their prime;
Each horse wore a string of bells
That made a merry chime.

The sleigh was brightly tended
In big red Christmas bows.
The horses moved with spirit
To Uncle's clicks and *whoa's*.
I remember there were icicles
Around each horse's nose,
Where fragrant breath came out in clouds
Through whiskers where it froze.

Once in the sleigh, our feet in hay,
We stayed as warm as toast.
A calfskin robe across our laps
Protected us the most.

The sleigh had runners smooth as glass
And, silent as a ghost,
We slid along over ice and snow,
And down each grade we'd coast.

The snow was white and clean and soft
And glittered in the sun.
The horses seemed to love it too,
And pranced along in fun.
That made the sleigh bells jingle so,
They soon began to run.
That sleigh just seemed to float along
Until five miles were done.

When Grandma met us at the door,
Each got a hug and kiss.
Our aunts and uncles, cousins too;
And oh, how we loved this!
A Christmas tree was shining there;
We heard the fireplace hiss
And smelled the baking mincemeat pies:
That was perfect bliss!

Photo Opposite
WINTER SLEIGHRIDE
Robert Cushman Hayes

What's an Old Card Anyway?

Phyllis C. Michael

Just look at this! It's quite a list!
I wonder, would one card be missed?
I surely can't take time to write
To all these folks! Besides, they might
Not ever think of me again —
That seems to be the way of men!
I think I'll send no more than six!
Then I'll have more time to fix
Some decorations and a tree
That's really beautiful to see.
I just can't rush around, I say,
And what's an old card anyway?

Oh, there's the mailman! Let me see!
Why, here's a card from Madge to me!
She says she often thinks of days
When we both rode in one-horse sleighs.
Ah yes, I too remember how;
But that, all that, is long gone now.

And here's a card from cousin Nell!
She says they're lonely, but all is well.
I haven't written once this year —
I should have though; she's such a dear.
And look at this card that's all in gold,
Expressing the words the angels told.
Ann says she hopes I'm truly blessed
With all that makes me happiest.

And who's this card from? Well, just look!
It's Sue! I see she even took
The time to say she baked a cake
Just like my mother used to make
At Christmastime! Well, bless her heart!
I guess it's time I got a start!
Now where's my pen and all those stamps?
I'm going to turn up all the lamps,
'Cause I have quite a lengthy list
And not *one person* shall be missed!

66

What Christmas Means to Me

Polly Perkins

It's a feeling of goodwill
Toward everyone I meet,
The crowd of smiling faces
Bustling in the street.

It is the Christmas carols
Sung with joyous sound,
The bright sparkling snowflakes
Floating to the ground.

It's the fragrant scent of pine
From the Christmas tree,
The happiness, the joy—
That's what Christmas means to me.

It's writing a Christmas letter
To a seldom-seen friend,
Wrapping precious gifts of love
For my family once again.

It's the shining eyes of children
When they hear the story old
Of the Christ Child in the manger,
The Wise Men who brought gold.

It's the sadness and the joy
When the angel on the tree
Seems to light a path to heaven—
That's what Christmas means to me.

Your Christmas Guest

James Dillet Freeman

Take time this Christmas Day to go
  A little way apart,
And with the hands of prayer prepare
  The house that is your heart.

Brush out the dusty fears; brush out
  The cobwebs of your care
Till in the house that is your heart,
  It's Christmas everywhere.

Light every window up with love
  And let your love shine through,
That they who walk outside may share
  The blessed light with you.

Then will the rooms with joy be bright,
  With peace the hearth be blessed;
And Christ Himself will enter in
  To be your Christmas guest.

Photo Opposite
CHURCH
OLD BENNINGTON, VERMONT
Gene Ahrens

Irving Berlin: The Man Who Gave Us *White Christmas* and *God Bless America*

"Irving Berlin has no place in American music. He *is* American music." This tribute is from Jerome Kern, one of America's foremost twentieth-century composers, to a colleague whose phenomenal career spans decades and whose contribution to American popular music remains unprecedented to date. He composed some three thousand songs in addition to the scores for twenty Broadway shows and seventeen Hollywood musicals. His influence carried to several generations of composers who emulated him. Yet Irving Berlin had no formal training nor any scientific understanding of music whatsoever. In fact, he never learned how to read music!

Born in Temun, Siberia, on May 11, 1888, Israel Baline was just four years old when his parents, Moses and Leah Baline, fled their native land in fear of a pogrom. With their eight children, the Balines set sail for America in the hopes that there they would find a better and more prosperous life. They found only tenement housing on New York's lower East Side where Moses worked as a supervisor in a slaughterhouse and young Israel (nicknamed "Izzy") became involved with the neighborhood street gangs. Eventually, enough money had

been saved for the family to afford a slightly better apartment; but in 1896, Moses Baline died.

It became increasingly difficult to support a fatherless family, so eight-year-old Izzy quit school in order to go out and earn money as a newspaper vendor. While selling papers on the streets of the Bowery, Izzy came into contact with all sorts of people. He was particularly fascinated by the waiters who made their living strolling between the tables in the saloons and singing to their customers. When he approached his mother with the suggestion that he, too, would like to become a "singing waiter," Leah Baline adamantly refused her son's request. The son of a devout Hebrew cantor singing popular tunes in Bowery saloons! Not to be deterred, however, fourteen-year-old Izzy Baline ran away from home in pursuit of a song career.

He landed his first permanent job as a waiter at Pelham's Cafe, a saloon in Chinatown run by Mike Salter. On his eight to six a.m. shift, Izzy combined singing with his regular duties. At first he depended upon the generosity of the customers who threw coins onto his tray. Later, Mike agreed to pay him a total of seven dollars per week for his singing.

A couple of years later Mike told his waiters that he wanted someone to come up with a clever, catchy tune to rival a recent hit composed by the pianist at Callaghan's, a competitor's saloon. Izzy and the resident pianist got together and between them composed *Marie from Sunny Italy*, a tune which appeared in print within just a few days; but due to a typographical error, the credits on the cover read: "Words by I. Berlin." From then on, the songwriter used no other name!

Meanwhile, Izzy discovered that he could pick out his own tunes by fingering the black keys of the piano. He had no concept of how to read or transcribe music, yet he could manage to provide simple accompaniment for his lyrics. Perhaps realizing his own potential, Izzy paid a visit to publisher Ted Snyder's office in Tin Pan Alley where, having dismissed both "Israel" and "Izzy" as names unbefitting a composer of popular music, he introduced himself to the general manager as Irving Berlin. Snyder hired him as a staff composer for twenty-five dollars a week. At the age of twenty-one, Berlin had finally found his niche!

About this time ragtime music began to reach its peak in America, and Berlin began to further develop the rag. Since Berlin had taught himself how to play on the black keys only, he purchased a special lever and attached it to the base of his keyboard. This lever, when shifted, converted the range of sound. After several initial attempts at ragtime tunes, he composed a song in 1911 that made musical history: *Alexander's Ragtime Band*.

Ragtime was joined by ballads in Berlin's repertoire only as a result of a devastating experience. In 1912, Berlin married Dorothy Goetz, the sister of his close friend, E. Ray Goetz. The newlyweds honeymooned in Cuba, but five months after their return to New York, Dorothy succumbed to typhoid fever contracted on the island. Miserable and depressed, Berlin could not bring himself to write any music so his brother-in-law took him on a cruise to Europe as therapy. After their return, Goetz suggested that the bereaved husband write from his emotions. Berlin followed this advice; and before long, his first real ballad, *When I Lost You*, appeared.

Although Berlin was prospering financially, since his wife's death there had been no love in his life apart from his music. However, in 1925, he met Ellin Mackay, socialite daughter of multi-millionaire Clarence Mackay. The romance had all the trappings of a fairy tale. When Mackay took his daughter to Europe, her absence prompted Berlin to compose the lovely ballads, *Always* and *Remember*. Following her return, the couple eloped on January 4, 1926. Four days later they sailed for Europe with the omnipresent piano in their stateroom.

On September 30, 1933, Moss Hart's show, *As Thousands Cheer*, opened for a triumphant run on Broadway. Berlin's musical score revealed that the master songwriter was once again back in form. One song in particular caught on. It was a tune Berlin had written in 1917 called *Smile and Show Your Dimple*. Sixteen years earlier the song had been an utter failure; but Berlin used it again, only changing the title to *Easter Parade*.

Berlin composed the scores for many of the best musical films of the 1930s. *Top Hat*, which featured his Academy Award winning song *Cheek to Cheek*, catapulted Fred Astaire and Ginger Rogers to fame. *Holiday Inn* introduced his famous *White Christmas*, which is still one of America's Yuletide favorites.

Berlin had a special knack for writing a song specifically for a given entertainer and adapting it to that singer's best style. When Kate Smith approached the composer in 1938 about writing a patriotic song which she could sing on her weekly radio show, Berlin went back to his extensive files and located a tune he thought might be the right thing. This song was a reject from his World War I musical, *Yip, Yip, Yaphank*. After making a few alterations, he submitted *God Bless America* to the singer. The song became our second anthem overnight, and Berlin requested that all the royalties from it be donated to the Boy Scouts, Girl Scouts, and Campfire Girls.

In July 1954, this man who had given so much of himself for his country received a gold medal especially appropriated for him by the United States Congress and presented by President Eisenhower. Inscribed upon the medal were these words: "In recognition of his services in composing many popular songs, including *God Bless America*." When asked which of his vast repertoire was his own personal favorite, the immigrant from Siberia replied: *God Bless America*.

Ellen Clark Deeb

From *FAMOUS AMERICAN COMPOSERS*, Copyright © 1977 by Ideals Publishing Corp., Nashville, TN 37214

San Antonio's *Las Posadas*

Christmas River

Each December, from ranches and farms and small towns throughout the Texas hill country, families come to San Antonio. They come to take part in a Christmas tradition as unique to the Southwest as the piñatas wreaths decorating their front doors. It is the night of *Las Posadas*, that most special of evenings when Mary and Joseph will come into the city in search of shelter.

For weeks San Antonio has prepared for the procession. The holiday season is announced at the end of November with the stringing of lights from trees along the San Antonio River. Draped from branches like Spanish moss, the lights cast their shimmering reflections on the water, giving the river a soft golden hue.

Booths along the banks offer handmade arts and crafts for sale during the River Walk Christmas Fair. Santa Claus arrives on a gaily decorated river barge, leading a string of other barges in a water-borne parade. And the San Antonio Garden Center welcomes guests into four elegant and lavishly decorated homes in its annual Christmas Pilgrimage.

A week before *Las Posadas* come *Fiestas Niño*. San Antonio dances in Market Square to mariachi bands as the aroma of traditional Mexican holiday foods hangs tantalizingly in the air. At the end of the week, family pets are brought to the Square as a priest from San Fernando Cathedral asks God's blessing on all His creatures.

But *Las Posadas*, a legacy of the time when

Texas was a raw frontier province on the edge of the Spanish Empire, remains the most beloved Christmas tradition. Today it is a tradition increasingly shared by others as visitors come to San Antonio from every state and several countries to join the celebration.

But no matter how many come or where they have come from, *Las Posadas* begins as it always has with a warm welcome and refreshments.

At the city's elegant *La Mansion del Rio* Hotel, plates of *bunuelos* greet those who have come to take part in the procession. They are Mexican cookies so light and delicate they seem in danger of crumbling into sugar dust in the children's eager hands. And there is hot chocolate flavored with the spices of the city's Hispanic heritage. Outside in the blue dusk hundreds of *luminarias*, candles in sand-weighted paper sacks, flicker along the banks of the San Antonio River.

In the shadows of *La Mansion's* graceful

Photos by San Antonio Convention & Visitor's Bureau/Al Randon

colonial archways, small candles are distributed and lit. Conversation and childish laughter give way to an expectant hush. A friar in the brown robes of the Franciscans offers a prayer. A hymn, sung in Spanish and as soft as bluebonnets tossing in the hill-country breeze, fills the air. The procession begins.

Guadalupe Plaza at Christmas

From the hotel, it winds along San Antonio's River Walk, the *Paseo del Rio*. Leading, a boy and a girl represent Mary and Joseph. Other San Antonio children gently carry a small clay image of the infant Jesus. And still others attend the Holy Family as shepherds and angels. Behind them, singing and sheltering their candles from the wind in cupped hands, follows the rest of the procession.

Rivercenter Christmas Pageant

Las Pastores—Guadalupe Plaza

Living Christmas Tree

They pass thousands of people lining the walk or looking down from balconies over the river. Others fill river barges tied up along the way or following close behind.

At a footbridge over the river, the procession pauses. On the bridge, carolers ask, "Who knocks at my door, so late in the night?"

From the darkness in the high clear voices of children comes the age-old plea. "We are pilgrims, without shelter, and we wish only a place to rest."

"There are no rooms; be gone," comes the answer from the bridge. "Go elsewhere and disturb me not again."

The procession moves on. A guitar adds its rich voice to the hymns and in the darkness the candles' tiny flames dance like fireflies.

A few minutes later the procession pauses at another bridge. And again Mary and Joseph are sent away into the night.

But soon they come to where the river bends

Las Posadas on the Riverwalk

near *la Villita* where *San Antonio de Bexar* was founded in 1718. On the outdoor stage of the Arneson River Theater, a manger with a straw floor waits. "Come into my humble home and welcome," sing the carolers there. "And may the Lord give shelter to my soul when I leave this world!"

Tenderly the image of the Christ Child is placed in a cradle. At long last the Holy Family has found refuge.

Suddenly mariachi music shatters the quiet in joyous celebration. Decorated egg shells, hollowed out and filled with confetti, break open in tiny blizzards of festive color. In *La Villita's* Maverick Plaza, gaudy piñatas bob and weave as blindfolded children swing at them with sticks. With a solid blow they break open, spilling their treats and toys onto the ground.

Across San Antonio, others celebrate Christmas in the ways of their ancestors who followed their dreams to Texas. The area's German settlers are remembered with *Die Deutsche Weihnachtsfeier*, a traditional candlelight service conducted entirely in German. At the Lila Cockrell Theater, the Nutcracker once again defeats the evil Mouse King. And madrigal singers from the University of Texas perform music both ancient and ageless at their annual Christmas Dinner.

For San Antonio, The closing of the Christmas season comes seven days into the new year. Not far from the city is Mission San José with its Rococo carvings and soaring bell tower. At the end of the first week in January, the passion play of *The*

Blessing of the Pets

Shepherds unfolds on the grounds of the mission.

First brought to San Antonio by the Franciscans to teach mission Indians, it is the classic struggle between good and evil. In simple and colorful folk costumes, players from Our Lady of Guadalupe Catholic Church tell the tale of shepherds on their way to honor the newborn Jesus. Lucifer, infuriated at Christ's coming, gathers his host of devils to bar the shepherds' way.

In the end, of course, the shepherds outwit and outfight the devils. Lucifer, hissing and grumbling, slinks away. And the shepherds continue their journey to present their humble gifts to the *Niño Jesús*.

Michael McKeever is a Contributing Editor of Country Inns *magazine and a frequent contributor to* Physicians Travel. *At journey's end, Michael enjoys returning home to Imperial Beach, California.*

Las Posadas on the Riverwalk

Photo Overleaf
CRATER LAKE
OREGON
Bob Clemenz Photography

Till Christmas Comes Again

Garnett Ann Schultz

It's time to tuck the tree away,
The ornaments and holly;
Time to wrap the silver bells,
Old Santa Claus so jolly,
The window stars and little elves,
Each wreath upon the door,
The manger scene and sleeping babe
Forgotten as before.

It's time to check the Christmas cards,
The greetings, oh, so dear,
The pleasant smiles they brought along
From friends both far and near,
To reminisce on days gone by—
The happy or the sad,
Still clinging to the beautiful
That made a moment glad.

The final days of one more year
With Christmas dreams come true,
When hearts then tuck away so much
The season brought to you.
Yet love and faith and gentle peace,
Goodwill and hope to men—
Do make them part of every day
Till Christmas comes again.

A New Beginning

Margaret Rorke

Every end's a new beginning
With another chance for winning—
A renewal of our energy and hope.
What is over only strengthens
The connecting link that lengthens
All of living with its duties and its scope.

So it is with marching seasons:
Each in sequence has its reasons
In the purpose and intention of the Lord.
Let us seize this as a sample—
A divinely sent example—
And perceive in new beginning—new reward.

A New Year Wish

Margaret Rorke

May the bright spots in the old year
Be but flickers in the dark
When compared with what the new year
Will enkindle with its spark.

Merry Christmas and a very Happy New Year from all of us at

ideals®

ideals
Celebrating Life's Most Treasured Moments